MEGA DINOSAURS
COLORING BOOK

JAN SOVAK

DOVER PUBLICATIONS
Garden City, New York

Copyright

Copyright © 2019 by Dover Publications
All rights reserved.

Bibliographical Note

Mega Dinosaurs Coloring Book is a new work,
first published by Dover Publications in 2019.

International Standard Book Number
ISBN-13: 978-0-486-83396-5
ISBN-10: 0-486-83396-8

Manufactured in the United States of America
83396804
www.doverpublications.com

Publisher's Note

Our fascination with dinosaurs never ends! No doubt, part of the appeal of these creatures lies in their enormous size—and in this fact-filled coloring book, you will learn about more than thirty "mega" dinosaurs. One of the largest of these, Diplodocus, may have weighed around 100 tons (200,000 pounds)! Even the smallest dinosaur featured in this book was thought to have weighed 2½ tons—a mere 5,000 pounds.

Dinosaurs lived on Earth between 225 and 65 million years ago. How do we gather our information about them? Every now and then, people have discovered fossilized remains of dinosaurs—bones and skeletons—that give us clues about their size and structure. Paleontologists (scientists who study fossils) build upon their knowledge each time new dinosaur bones are found. Dinosaur remains have been found in places as distant from each other as Texas and China, and Argentina and Egypt!

The dimensions for each "mega" dinosaur are given (height and length), as well as its approximate weight. Other details will give you a better picture of the kind of life the dinosaur lived—near water or in the desert, for example, and the kind of food it ate. The illustrations show the dinosaur's habitat. Artist Jan Sovak has even provided an image of a human next to each dinosaur to emphasize just how *enormous* these creatures were! Enjoy coloring each detailed picture as you read about its characteristics and unique features.

Acrocanthosaurus. Length: 38 ft.; Height: 12 ft.; Weight: 8 tons. Evidence of one of the largest *theropods* ("beast-footed" dinosaurs) has been found in North America, mostly in Texas, Oklahoma, and Wyoming. However, its teeth have been located as far away as Maryland, suggesting that this huge predator roamed much of the continent. A bone of a *sauropod* ("lizard-hipped" dinosaur) bearing the marks of Acrocanthosaurus's teeth appears to prove that this giant predator hunted some of the biggest dinosaurs of its time.

Allosaurus. Length: 30 ft.; Height: 12 ft.; Weight: 2.5 tons. Based on fossil finds in the Morrison Formation in North America in Colorado, Montana, and New Mexico, it appears that Allosaurus hunted in packs in order to conquer large prey. Recent findings of very large animals show that they could grow to an enormous size. This "mega" dinosaur has also been identified in Africa, Australia, and Europe.

Amphicoelias. Length: 190 ft.; Height: 30 ft. at pelvis; Weight: 135 tons. We know about this creature from only one vertebra, a partial femur bone that survived in a detailed drawing by paleontologist E. Cope, who discovered the bones in 1877. If what we know is correct, Amphicoelias would be the biggest animal known to have inhabited Earth—so big that some paleontologists question how it could function at all.

Carcharodontosaurus. Length: 44 ft.; Height: 12 ft.; Weight: up to 15 tons. Another of the very large predators with a massive head and neck, Carcharodontosaurus hunted in the desert region known today as the Sahara. It was calculated that Carcharodontosaurus, because of the massive muscles in its neck and upper torso, could use its jaws to pick up an animal weighing up to 1,000 pounds and hold it in the air.

Cedarpelta. Length: 20 ft.; Height: 10 ft.; Weight: 4.5 tons. Found in a small quarry in the Cedar Mountain region, Utah, this large *ankylosaur* ("armored dinosaur") differed somewhat from others of this dinosaur group. It did not have the typical "beak" for cutting down tough vegetation and did not possess the typical club at the end of its tail.

Chilantaisaurus. Length: 43 ft.; Height: 11 ft.; Weight: 4.5 tons. Fossil remains of this large predatory theropod have been discovered in Mongolia, China, and Russia. Not much is known about this dinosaur, but Chilantaisaurus must had been almost as big as T. Rex, with unusually long claws that made it quite unique in this class of predatory dinosaurs!

Dacentrurus. Length: 26 ft.; Height: 12 ft.; Weight: 5.5 tons. This was a large *stegosaurid* ("having spikes and plates along its back"), almost identical to Stegosaurus; however, it differed from that dinosaur in the arrangement of its spikes and plates. Dacentrurus lived in Europe at a time when "mega" dinosaurs such as Allosaurus and Poekilosaurus were the chief predatory dinosaurs. Perhaps for that reason stegosaurids developed such extensive defensive armor.

Deinocheirus. Length: 36 ft.; Height: 12 ft. at hips; Weight: 6.4 tons. This dinosaur had enormous forelegs with long claws. Deinocheirus was found in the Nemegt Formation in Mongolia. It took many decades to classify this animal—after the discovery of the fossilized remains of other animals and after locating important parts that had been sold to private collectors in Europe, it was established that Deinocheirus was an unusual *ornithomimosaurus* ("ostrich" dinosaur) that lived on a diet of plants. Some Deinocheirus bones had markings left by Tarbosaurus (related to Tyrannosaurus Rex) teeth.

Diplodocus. Length: 110 ft.; Height: 12 ft. at shoulders; Weight: 90–100 tons. One of the earliest dinosaurs found, Diplodocus was discovered and named in 1878 by Othniel Charles Marsh; it is one of the longest dinosaurs we know of. Its unusually lengthy and slender tail probably was used as a defensive weapon against predators. Although many skeletons of Diplodocus have been discovered, none contained a skull, so we can only guess what Diplodocus looked like by comparing it to other related species.

Dreadnoughtus. Length: 85 ft.; Height: 25 ft.; Weight: 42 tons. This dinosaur was found in Argentina in 2005. Its skeleton is almost complete, and several bones carry signs of scavenging by predators. Even small teeth belonging to smaller teropods were found nearby. It is believed that this dinosaur died of natural causes, and small predatory dinosaurs discovered the body later. This plant-eating dinosaur's name means "fears nothing," no doubt due to its great size.

Edmontosaurus. Length: 39 ft.; Height: 16 ft.; Weight: 10 tons. One of the largest of the *hadrosaur* ("duck-billed") dinosaurs, Edmontosaurus lived in North America in packs that might have numbered in the hundreds. It could grow to an enormous size, sometimes up to 39 feet in length and weighing more than 10 tons. Edmontosaurus is important, as it was one of the first dinosaur fossil discoveries. Mummified remains of this species have been found along with preserved skin, beaks, and other important parts that usually have not been preserved.

Giganotosaurus. Length: 44 ft.; Height: 12 ft.; Weight: 8 tons. This large predator from Argentina typically was suited for hunting down equally large prey. Giganotosaurus has been calculated to have reached a speed of 31 mph! Based on findings of Mapusaurus and Albertosaurus fossils, it has been suggested that these enormous theropods hunted together in large packs. Despite their size, their brains were only about the size of a banana!

Giraffatitan. Length: 72 ft.; Height: 40 ft.; Weight: 24–38 tons. The first description of this giant sauropod was devised in 1914, based on a partial skeleton found in Tanzania, Africa. Later on, the creature was renamed, as more fossilized remains were discovered. Giraffatitan is one of the tallest dinosaurs, and due to the structure of its skull, some scientists believe that it might have had a trunk similar to that of the modern elephant!

Magnapaulia. Length: 49 ft.; Height: 14 ft.; Weight: 12 tons. One of the largest hadrosaurs, Magnapaulia's fossilized remains suggest that it lived near the water and probably spent considerable time in it as well. The suggestion came from the fact that the remains included a healed femur fracture, which some scientists believe would have been a fatal injury if it had taken place on land (in the water, the injury would have healed, as no stress would have been placed on the injury).

Mamenchisaurus. Length: 115 ft.; Height: 30 ft.; Weight: 70 tons. Named after the area of China where it was discovered, this dinosaur had an extremely long neck, up to 58 feet, constituting half the length of Mamenchisaurus's body! One of this dinosaur's cervical ribs measured 13½ feet—the longest bone of any land animal that we know of!

Mapusaurus. Length: 40 ft.; Height: 14 ft.; Weight: 3.5 tons. A relative of Giganotosaurus, this large predator was discovered in Argentina. Fossilized remains of at least seven other dinosaurs were found at the same location, suggesting that even "mega" dinosaurs could have hunted in packs!

Notocolossus. Length: 90 ft.; Height: 26 ft.; Weight: 60 tons. Notocolossus was discovered in Argentina in 2015. Given its massive size, Notocolossus is one of the largest known *titanosaurids* (long-necked dinosaurs). It weighed more than ten elephants! Notocolossus lived in the same region as other huge sauropods such as Dreadnoughtus, as well as giant predators such as Giganotosaurus and Mapusaurus.

Oxalaia. Length: 45 ft.; Height: unknown; Weight: 7.7 tons. The largest theropod found in Brazil, Oxalaia is believed by some scientists to have been a relative of Spinosaurus. The environment of Oxalaia was also almost identical to the one inhabited by Spinosaurus, in what is today North Africa. Surrounded by a rain forest, Spinosaurids lived much the same way as modern crocodiles, catching fish but also opportunistically feeding on animals that had come to drink water or had perished nearby.

Pachyrhinosaurus. Length: 23 ft.; Height: 11 ft.; Weight: 4.5 tons. Pachyrhinosaurus was a large dinosaur that had unusual bony structures, called *bosses*, on the front part of its skull. These structures varied from each other, probably to identify each animal. In northern Canada, a large "bone bed" was discovered containing numerous adults, juveniles, and babies, suggesting that Pachyrhinosaurus lived in a herd and cared for its offspring. Three different species of Pachyrhinosaurus have been identified.

Paralititan. Length: 80 ft.; Height: 28 ft.; Weight: 65 tons. Paralititan was discovered in Egypt. Its fossilized remains were found alongside fossilized mangrove trees and leaves, providing clues to the environment in which this dinosaur lived. The body of a Paralititan might also have been deposited there by flooding waters or a tidal wave. Paralititan's body displayed signs of having been scavenged by predators.

Parasaurolophus. Length: 30 ft.; Height: 14 ft.; Weight: 2.8 tons. Parasaurolophus was a large hadrosaur that lived in today's North America. It is one of the rarest hadrosaurs and certainly one that had unusual head "ornaments." These were typical for this group of dinosaurs and provided not only a way to distinguish between males and females, but also served as a tool for social communication, similar to modern animals such as deer and elks.

Saurophaganax. Length: 40 ft.; Height: 14 ft.; Weight: 3.5 tons. Saurophaganax was one of the largest predators in North America. Its fragmentary fossilized remains were found in the Morrison Formation in Oklahoma. In recent years, a new specimen was discovered in New Mexico. Saurophaganax lived alongside sauropods such as Apatosaurus, Barosaurus, Brontosaurus, and Camarasaurus.

Sauroposeidon. Length: 112 ft.; Height: 59 ft.; Weight: 62–72 tons. With a height reaching almost 60 feet, Sauroposeidon is the tallest dinosaur known to us. It lived in the same region as the large predator Acrocanthosaurus and probably was the only predator to hunt such a huge prey. Sauroposeidon and Acrocanthosaurus lived in the delta of a river that extended from the Gulf of Mexico to Oklahoma at that time.

Shantungosaurus. Length: 54 ft.; Height: 15 ft.; Weight: 18 tons. One of the largest of the hadrosaurs, Shantungosaurus possessed a skull more than 5 feet long, and was believed to have had close to 1,500 small teeth packed in its jaws. Because of similarities between the North American Edmontosaurus and the Chinese Shantungosaurus, a theory exists about dinosaur migrations from continent to continent—similarities between some species of dinosaurs support this.

Spinosaurus. Length: 59 ft.; Height: 15 ft. at highest vertebra; Weight: up to 10 tons. Spinosaurus was a huge predator with a snout resembling a crocodile's, as well as a massive sail-like structure on its back. It is possible that Spinosaurus, similarly to a crocodile, lived an aquatic or partly aquatic life, eating mainly a diet of fish. Its fossilized remains were found in what are today Egypt and Morocco, on the shores of a vast but shallow sea and in the deltas of a river.

33

Stegosaurus. Length: 29 ft.; Height: 15 ft.; Weight: 7.7 tons. One of the best-known dinosaurs—as well as the largest of all stegosaurs—Stegosaurus lived alongside large sauropods such as Apatosaurus, Brachiosaurus, and the predatory teropods Allosaurus and Ceratosaurus. Its spikes clearly were defensive weapons, but the role of its plates still are the subject of debate among researchers.

Suchomimus. Length: 36 ft.; Height: 12 ft.; Weight: 5 tons. Discovered in Niger, Africa, by American paleontologists, Suchomimus is a dinosaur whose behavior is similar to that of a modern crocodile. It lived on the shores of a shallow body of water, and its diet consisted mainly of fish. However, with more than 100 teeth in its jaws, this dinosaur might have preyed upon smaller dinosaurs as well as other animals, as the remains in its stomach contents suggest.

Supersaurus. Length: 112 ft.; Height: 30 ft.; Weight: 40 tons. Discovered in Colorado in 1972, this plant-eating dinosaur was related to Diplodocus and Apatosaurus. However, its skeletal remains were found along with another giant sauropod, Brachiosaurus, making it difficult to identify which bones belonged to which creature. Fortunately, years later another Supersaurus skeleton was discovered in Wyoming, thus helping to correct the identification errors that were made in collecting the original species in Colorado.

Tarchia. Length: 26 ft.; Height: 8 ft.; Weight: 4.5 tons. Tarchia was one of the largest ankylosaurs—the remains of several of these animals were found in the Nemegt Basin in Mongolia. Tarchia lived in very dry, desertlike conditions and was well adapted for surviving in such an environment. It had a large beak for cutting down tough vegetation for food. The discovery of a Tarchia skull in which a large Tarbosaurus tooth was embedded suggests that Tarchia was the Tarbosaurus's prey.

Titanoceratops. Length: 23 ft.; Height: 11 ft.; Weight: 7.3 tons. Its massive skull reaching almost 9 feet in length, Titanoceratops ("titanic horn face") had the longest skull of any known land animal. This horned inhabitant of North America—in what is modern-day New Mexico—was a plant-eater.

38

Torosaurus. Length: 30 ft.; Height: 12 ft.; Weight: 6.5 tons. Like Titanoceratops, Torosaurus possessed one of the largest skulls of any known land animal. The skull had two large horns above the eye orbits but a relatively small nasal horn. The frill on the skull was one of the biggest among *ceratopsian* ("horned-face") dinosaurs. Recent studies pointed out the similarities between Torosaurus and Triceratops, and some paleontologists believe that Torosaurus could be an adult Triceratops!

Turiasaurus. Length: 120 ft.; Height: 21 ft. at shoulder blades; Weight: 48 tons. Turiasaurus is the largest dinosaur ever discovered in Europe. It was discovered in Spain, where initially only a few fragmentary bones were uncovered, but later on additional fossilized bones were found and a complete skeleton was reconstructed. Turiasaurus's head was unusually small for such a large animal. Fossils of juveniles were also found within the bone bed.

Tyrannosaurus Rex. Length: 40 ft.; Height: 12 ft. at hips; Weight: 9 tons. Tyrannosaurus Rex, popularly known as T. Rex, is one of the best-known dinosaurs. Its skeletal remains have been discovered throughout the western part of North America, and some of the skeletons have been preserved complete to the last bone. One of the largest predators of all time, T. Rex possessed a stronger bite force than even larger predators such as Giganotosaurus.

Tyrannotitan. Length: 40 ft.; Height: 13 ft.; Weight: 7 tons. A relatively recent find, Tyrannotitan was discovered in Chubut province, Argentina, in 2005. It is one of the earliest "mega" dinosaurs known to us and was related to other giant predators like Giganotosaurus and Mapusaurus. Tyrannotitan could reach a larger size than T. Rex and probably specialized in hunting down huge sauropods.

Wuerhosaurus. Length: 21 ft.; Height: 10 ft.; Weight: 4 tons. This dinosaur was related to the famed Stegosaurus but lived much later in the region that is now modern-day China. Not much is known about Wuerhosaurus, as its skeletal remains are fragmentary and poorly preserved. We do know that it was a very large size for a stegosaurid but stood a bit lower, perhaps as a result of an adaptation for browsing for food in the lower parts of vegetation.

43

Index

Acrocanthosaurus 2	Pachyrhinosaurus 26
Allosaurus 4	Paralititan 28
Amphicoelias 6	Parasaurolophus 29
Carcharodontosaurus 8	Saurophaganax 30
Cedarpelta 10	Sauroposeidon 31
Chilantaisaurus 11	Shantungosaurus 32
Dacentrurus 12	Spinosaurus 33
Deinocheirus 14	Stegosaurus 34
Diplodocus 15	Suchomimus 35
Dreadnoughtus 16	Supersaurus 36
Edmontosaurus 17	Tarchia 37
Giganotosaurus 18	Titanoceratops 38
Giraffatitan 19	Torosaurus 39
Magnapaulia 20	Turiasaurus 40
Mamenchisaurus 21	Tyrannosaurus Rex 41
Mapusaurus 22	Tyrannotitan 42
Notocolossus 24	Wuerhosaurus 43
Oxalaia 25	